Mar 2014

D1511919

DIGITAL CAREER BUILDING™

CAREER BUILDING THROUGH

USING DIGITAL STORY TOOLS

JASON GLASER

ROSEN
PUBLISHING®

New York

Published in 2014 by The Rosen Publishing Group, Inc.
29 East 21st Street, New York, NY 10010

First Edition

Library of Congress Cataloging-in-Publication Data

Glaser, Jason.
Career building through using digital story tools/Jason Glaser.—
First edition.
   pages cm.—(Digital career building)
Includes bibliographical references and index.
ISBN 978-1-4777-1722-6 (library binding)—ISBN 978-1-4777-1735-6
(pbk.)—ISBN 978-1-4777-1736-3 (6-pack)
1. Digital storytelling—Juvenile literature. 2. Storytelling—Juvenile
literature. I. Title.
LB1042.G57 2014
372.67'7—dc23

                                                              2013013962

Manufactured in the United States of America

CPSIA Compliance Information: Batch #W14YA: For further information, contact Rosen Publishing, New York,
New York, at 1-800-237-9932.

CONTENTS

CHAPTER ONE

OLD SKILLS, NEW TOOLS

In 2011, the last factory in the world dedicated to making typewriters closed down. That story appeared in newspapers, but most people who read about it did so online. News Web sites and social media discussed it. Comments sprang from smartphones, laptops, and tablet PCs. It reminded people how publishing had changed since the days of ink ribbon typewriters.

Technology has changed the way people engage in news and entertainment. Pocket mobile devices are capable of storing the text for any book you might want to read. Teenagers can view films from other countries and post reviews online while riding the bus. The ultra-connected nature of our world means that news events unfold on the Internet in real time. What's more, the way news is shared and develops online often impacts the story itself.

A New Face on an Old Tradition

Storytelling is, at its root, a social tradition. Traditional storytellers were performers, telling tales for an audience. The craft was as much about performance as content. The digital age advances many of these elements, including audience reaction. Through the Internet and social media, the words people write and the images they share bring near-immediate feedback. Readers comment, criticize, share, or even build upon those works. Touching stories grow rapidly, becoming "viral."

For better or for worse, today's teens find themselves already in the public eye. They scatter pieces of their lives to dozens or maybe hundreds of "friends" on Facebook or "followers" on Twitter. They're never more than a cell phone's distance from a camera. More than ever, digitally connected teens are budding characters in their own narratives.

With this native understanding of social technology and audience comes opportunity. Ad companies, film production studios, game designers, and publishers constantly wrestle with ways to appeal to a Web savvy audience. A person who understands how to communicate an idea or a story through such media has a very valuable skill in many employers' eyes. As storytelling tradition is deeply rooted in all cultures and understood even by children, those primary skills develop early. A job telling stories for art,

Passing notes has taken a leap forward in technology now that teens can share text and other media through connected devices.

profit, or both may be closer than many young people realize.

Pixel Pages

As teens' access to tablets and smartphones increases, so does their access to and dependence on digital media. For today's students, the concept of bringing home a "page-turner" has changed greatly. In 2011, *School Library Journal* reported that 71 percent of high school libraries were offering digital editions of books, or e-books. Over half of middle schools offered them as well. Students often don't need to visit the library to get them. Many libraries

The Pioneer

Dana Winslow Atchley III is the person most often credited for sparking the digital storytelling movement. A performance artist and video producer, Atchley had been combining different media together in his performances since the 1970s. Computers let Atchley deliver all of his media with one easy-to-use tool. He shared his vast collection of photographs, audio recordings, videotapes, and art with audiences in a performance he called "Next Exit" in the 1990s.

Atchley's shows evoked the familiar scenario of telling stories around a campfire. He even projected a digital campfire onto a small screen at his feet. Images and movies played on a larger screen behind him. No two performances were the same. His stories were "packed" into digital suitcases on-screen that he opened using a wireless mouse onstage. He went from story to story as the moment moved him or based on audience response.

The techniques Atchley developed for his performances proved effective for more than art. Companies such as Coca-Cola and Apple hired Atchley to help them express ideas and tell stories about their products. He tried to teach others that a presentation should be about more than giving information. It should provide information in a meaningful way.

Unfortunately, Atchley died in 2000 at the age of fifty-nine. He would not be able to expand people's vision of digital storytelling by using the new technologies that followed. Many people believe that advertising, corporate presentations, and even Web design would be very different today had he lived.

allow patrons to remotely download digital copies of books directly onto reading devices or computers.

Additionally, in early 2013, the Association of American Publishers (AAP) estimated that e-book sales made up 22.5 percent—or more than a fifth—of all book sales. The young adult market in particular is growing quickly as teenagers comfortable with technology race to finish "must-read" series. While school libraries, local libraries, and even bookstores may not be able to keep copies on their shelves, digital files are always available from online retailers.

Subscription media has found some digital success. One of the largest magazine publishers, Hearst Magazines International, claimed eight hundred thousand digital subscribers at the end of 2012. A letter to employees stated that soon a majority of its customers would view its publications online. The same year, the long-standing print magazine *Newsweek* stopped printing in the United States and became an online-only publication.

In October 2012, digital comic distributor ComiXology trumpeted its one hundred millionth down-loaded comic. This signaled a huge change for the comic book industry. In the past, digital comics were just scanned pages shared on the Internet that cut into sales. Today, companies such as Marvel and Dark Horse Comics produce their own digital subscriptions and special "motion comics" for screen viewing.

The digital shift has been rougher on newspapers, the traditional source for current information on many subjects. Facebook has eclipsed the "society pages." Box scores are updated in real time on sports Web sites. Even

 The landscape of electronic reading devices and methods is still in its early stages, but the market is growing rapidly.

the daily crossword can be done online or passed over for a few minutes spent on Farmville. Rather than a pre-selected mix of news items bound to a newspaper, readers visit Web aggregators such as Digg and Reddit to keep up on the latest events.

One positive note for papers is that timely or well-written articles can actually reach a wider audience than ever before. Online stories shared on social sites are seen by people across the country and around the world. Touching tales or horrible crimes often reach beyond the paper's subscribers once they are copied and shared electronically.

A less-than-honest form of digital storytelling appears in chain e-mails and other Internet spam. Crafty writers tell an amazing or emotional story and ask people to share it or pass it on to others. Nearly all of these "please share" stories are fabricated. Many are designed to see how big an audience they can get. Others try to manipulate a reader's thoughts or actions. The worst of them try to trick readers into giving out money or personal information.

A Byte of the Pie

Whether in print or online, profiting from stories is often a triangular relationship. Quality content and presentation can draw readers who might pay the publisher or content provider to read or subscribe. However, the revenue from paying readers is small compared to the money earned from advertisers who want to reach these readers. Web sites or magazines with lots of readers can get paid well to host ads alongside their stories.

Facebook alone boasts nearly a billion active users per month. Many of those eyeballs belong to teenagers. In fact, Facebook hosts an estimated nine out of ten teens. Teens are a target demographic, so Facebook is one of many prime digital targets for rapidly increasing advertising dollars. *Bloomberg Businessweek* estimates that digital advertising revenue is a tenth of that for print. However, while print advertising dollars have

 The digital age has created "freemium" markets, in which some content is free but premium perks must be purchased.

stayed flat, the magazine predicts money spent on digital ads will double within a few years.

 Social media is a rapidly changing environment. Within a few years, newer and better tools will probably emerge. The programs and sites in this book represent what is possible in storytelling, rather than what tools one must use.

Digital advertising rates are based on how many people view the ad or click on it. News sites, Web comics, casual game sites, and online journals are all equally appealing. Any site with content that draws thousands of daily visits can benefit from ad revenue.

Digital storytelling is accessible to everyone because the most common creation tools are freely available at sites that work with video, audio, and pictures. Sites such as YouTube and Flickr offer their services and content for free. Advertisers pay them to reach the millions of people who visit every day. Such sites are like vast virtual galleries in which all can share their work in exchange for letting companies advertise alongside it.

Not all digital storytelling tools operate that way to make money. A number of businesses offer paid services helpful to digital storytellers. Companies might offer on-demand publishing or formatting of stories into various e-book formats. Freelance editors, writers, and illustrators who can help with a project can be found through online networking services. Web sites such as Xtranormal, which helps users turn text into a movie, offer free animation tools but charge for the premium elements.

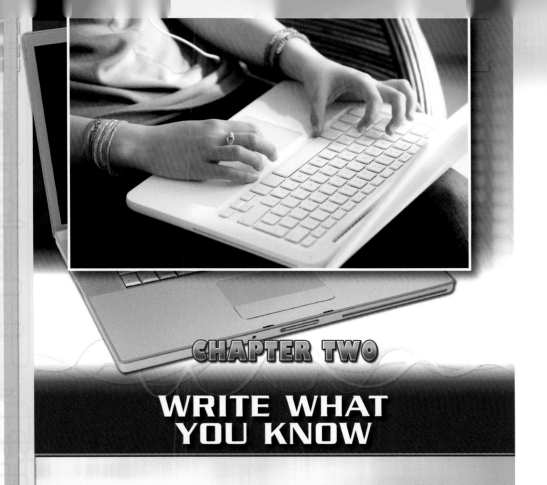

CHAPTER TWO

WRITE WHAT YOU KNOW

A common bit of advice to writers has been "write what you know." This carries the belief that experience is the key. It suggests that younger people with less life experience behind them have little to write about. It also forgets that younger people can write for their peers. Both Christopher Paolini and Alexandra Adornetto became famous for writing fantasy books for teens as teens. In fact, creativity, hard work, and practice are the most critical tools of any storyteller. In addition, understanding the nature of modern storytelling can make young people well prepared for a full, satisfying career.

Success stories like Amanda Hocking's are the exception, but the opportunity to strike it big is certainly there for others.

14

New Possibilities

Amanda Hocking probably represents everything traditional publishers fear about the future. Hocking published her paranormal romance books as e-books by herself. They caught the interest of young adults comfortable with using technology. Her books went on to sell over a million copies on Amazon, with little more than word of mouth for advertising.

Selling directly to consumers is a thriving model for a number of sequential artists—or graphic storytellers— too. In newspapers, artists' and cartoonists' work is small, static, and often colorless. On the Web, comic artists are free to experiment with color, size, motion, and Web programming tricks to help tell their stories. Pete Abrams has been doing a lighthearted story-driven daily comic called *Sluggy Freelance* on the Internet since 1997. So far his daily strip has been made into more than ten volumes, sold as books.

Such possibilities are not reserved for fiction. Imagination and creativity extend to all forms of prose and expression.

Share and Share Alike

The operating theme of digital storytelling is "share." Content creators share their work easily and instantly over the Web without having to copy or print it. They can send or announce it through e-mail or put it out on the Web for people to find. The ability to share work digitally brings with it greater opportunities for audience response. Feedback in the form of comments, replies, responses, or additional content builds upon the initial experience and creates deep, personal connections. Digital storytelling is often incomplete without some form of interaction.

Short for "Web log," a blog is an ongoing interaction with readers through content organized by date. It is a workable sharing method for many types of content. Each new entry appears foremost on the Web page, with older entries available for further reading. Some blog posts are mostly text, with little imagery, while others might be daily photographs with small amounts of text. Readers are almost always invited to take part in the unfolding conversation triggered by each new entry. WordPress, Blogger, and LiveJournal—all free tools—are common entry points for new bloggers.

Bloggers must be careful about what they reveal. Young people who reveal too much about themselves can become targets. This is why many cautious teen journalists do not use their real names, post pictures of themselves, or talk about where they live or go to school.

Journalism 2.0

Sometimes the line between blogging and journalism becomes blurred. Both bloggers and journalists may report on current events. Traditional journalists try to keep themselves out of the story. They report without attempting to influence readers. Bloggers usually make themselves the subject, or at least color the topic with their personal thoughts and opinions.

Top-Tier Teens

Teenagers' use of blogs has decreased since 2006, when an estimated one in four online teens had tried creating a blog. However, a number have followed through with their commitment to providing continuing content and have built a following. Successful teen bloggers include:

- **Tavi Gevinson**. At the top of the list of teenage successes is probably Tavi Gevinson. Tavi started her fashion blog, *Style Rookie*, at age eleven. By 2012, at sixteen, *Huffington Post* named the insightful and entertaining teen one of the most amazing young people of the year. Her online magazine for girls, called *Rookie*, launched in September 2011. It reached a million views within five days.

- **Stephen Yellin**. Stephen Yellin was covering politics before he could vote. His well-researched, extensive coverage earned him an invitation to attend and blog about the 2004 Democratic National Convention at age sixteen. In doing so, he

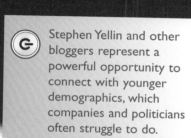

Stephen Yellin and other bloggers represent a powerful opportunity to connect with younger demographics, which companies and politicians often struggle to do.

-became the youngest journalist to cover a national political convention. In college, he won first place for editorial writing from the New Jersey Press Association. He currently serves on a number of political action teams and advisory boards.

- **Malala Yousafzai.** The country of Pakistan is in constant struggle between the Pakistani government and armed rebels known as the Taliban. In areas they control, the Taliban have opposed education for women. In 2009, the BBC hosted a blog by eleven-year-old Malala Yousafzai, a headmaster's daughter seeking education for herself and other girls. As a public figure, Malala became a target for the Taliban. In October 2012, Taliban gunmen stopped her on her way to school and shot her. She miraculously survived the attack and still fights for increased education for girls in Pakistan and around the world.

Bloggers and journalists use many of the same tools. Twitter, in particular, has become a valuable tool for both. Its 140-character limit is popular among "microbloggers" and lets reporters state the key details of a story. Often including a shortened link to the larger story, journalists' tweets serve as a means to inform interested readers and help them navigate to the expanded story.

Both bloggers and journalists use word processing programs to write their stories. They may also use blogging tools to file their stories and add links and images. Network access points give both kinds of writers the ability to work nearly anywhere. In addition to writing and editing capabilities, many portable digital devices have cameras or even microphones that can add extra content to a story.

Cultural Connections

World travelers have also been empowered by the new media. In the past, some documenting could certainly be done during a trip. However, journal entries, photographs, souvenirs, and notes taken abroad had to wait before the traveler could share them with others. Those at home had to settle for a phone call or a postcard in the mail to hear how things were going.

Today, technology brings followers into the travel story. A traveler can log entries, post video or audio from a trip, and upload pictures from a phone or digital camera. With GPS-enabled devices, the traveler can interact further by "checking in" at locations with programs such as Foursquare. Geocaching

Today's smartphones not only help world travelers find their way but also allow them to share a trip with friends and family in real time.

software can share the coordinates where the traveler finds specially placed objects left by others or leaves something new for future treasure hunters. "Augmented reality" programs on GPS- and camera-enabled smartphones let travelers leave messages and information for fellow users who might someday stand on that exact spot.

One thing technology can't do is give a reader a delicious taste over the Internet. Food lovers must continue to trust visitors' reviews. However, technology has given foodies their own interactions. A person can snap and upload a picture of the appetizer before the main course arrives. On the side, one might add a link to the nutritional content and a recipe showing how to make a similar dish at home.

The tools are so simple that a child can use them, and they have. As a nine-year-old, Martha Payne decided to be her school's food critic. Her blog showed pictures of the food and commented on its taste and appearance. By looking at student lunches this way, Martha made a statement about their quality. It even caught the attention of television star and chef Jamie Oliver. Within weeks of beginning her blog, the school began offering better, healthier options.

Social Media Journalism

In some places, digital storytelling is the only way a story can get out. There are many troubled places where the news is limited. Social media journalists there are able to reach the outside world in key moments.

Sometimes these moments are accidental. Pakistanis Sohaib Athar and Mohsin Shah both reported online about noisy gunfire and a helicopter strike nearby. It turned out they had accidentally covered the raid that killed Osama bin Laden.

In 2011, the power Moammar Gadhafi had held for decades over Libya was slipping. Seventeen-year-old Atem Shembech and her friends began to report about their lives amid the change. Their physical newspaper, the *Berenice Post*, was written and distributed in both Arabic and English. Through Facebook and other outlets, the *Berenice Post* published images and information that captured the chaos and aftermath of the uprising.

Social journalists are everywhere. CNN regularly features stories, videos, and editorials from "iReporters." These are everyday people whose added coverage of newsworthy events provides perspective that CNN's reporters could not possibly gather alone. Numerous iReporters have used their stories to successfully work toward internships or jobs at newspapers, TV stations, and CNN itself.

Watch Me Now

Few people understand the possibilities of digital story-telling like Felicia Day. In 2007, Day created a Web series about a team of online gamers who finally decide to meet in real life. *The Guild* drew in over four million viewers and was picked up by Microsoft for several more seasons. Day branched out into more Web series, Web

Felicia Day's success with her award-winning video blog, *The Flog*, led her to collaborate in creating Geek and Sundry, an Internet entertainment channel featuring original Web series programming.

movies, comics, and prerecorded talk shows known as podcasts.

Day's successful projects take advantage of several features of digital storytelling. First, high-speed Internet access lets people download and store large amounts of information. Along with listening to music and radio, people can watch high-definition movies and television-style shows online. Users can enjoy them wherever they are, whenever they want. This process, sometimes called time shifting, means no one has to miss an episode of a favorite show. So many people watch TV shows online that companies such as Amazon and Netflix have taken notice. Both now produce original shows and movies viewable only on their own services.

Film and music lovers benefit also. The opportunities available to discuss and share music and cinema have grown tremendously. People can access media and share their opinions from around the world. They no longer have to import CDs and movies or travel to other places to hear songs from new bands.

Game On

Interactive games have been a means of storytelling for quite some time. The earliest computer games were text-only games, or included pictures only as support. Players typed in simple commands such as "pick up the torch." A simple form, interactive fiction (IF) can be inspiring art. Adam Cadre's mind-bending work *Photopia*, first released in 1998, is considered a groundbreaking work in this genre.

One can experience Adam Cadre's *Photopia* and other examples of his games and interactive fiction at http://adamcadre.ac/if.html.

Few people think of video games as having a story, and many games don't. But some provide characters and stories as thoughtful and touching as movie plots. Haunting tales unfold in games like *Braid*, *Limbo*, and *Machinarium*. Telltale's game *The Walking Dead* won over eighty awards in 2012. Critics were amazed at how well it expressed the same depth of emotions as the show it was based on.

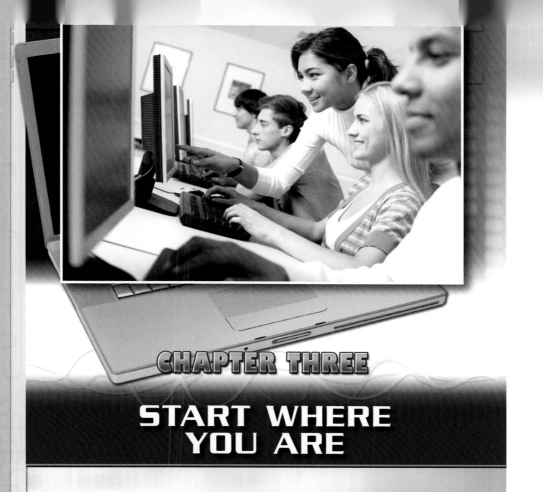

CHAPTER THREE

START WHERE YOU ARE

Today's teens don't usually think of a movie or a music album as a physical object. Rather, it is more of an experience. A physical disc is often used only long enough to rip the data to a computer or an iPod. Because data can be duplicated easily, works can be shared, altered, or combined at will. This data flexibility has inspired a remix culture. Music tracks are reshaped into club mixes or brought together in mash-ups. Video footage and striking images can be overlaid with text to create social commentary or humor pieces. Some of them blossom into Internet memes—or ideas that spread throughout the culture—almost overnight.

Teens in this mind-set can creatively mix elements from their classes, hobbies, and interests. They can take their strengths and share them in a way that connects with people. Digital technology provides more ways to tell stories and express ideas than ever before.

Hands On

For teens who want to be digital storytellers, schools can be helpful even outside of the regular school day. Computers and high-speed Internet connections are available in many homes, but not in all. For those who don't have them, or whose usage is limited, a computer lab is a great resource. Even an hour spent working before or after school on a regular basis can result in a lot of material over time.

School computer labs often have high-end software for design, writing, and editing that home computers don't. Lab assistants can help students use the software effectively. Computers in the school library or a writing center can be useful, too. One can write and do research at the same time, or use books on writing for story ideas.

Programs you find useful in the computer lab may be cheaper to buy than you might think. Many software companies offer academic pricing to students and teachers. Buying academic software licenses while in school can save hundreds of dollars on software costs.

G- Digital tools are flexible enough and precise enough to allow people to create and draw directly on the screen.

Game Changer

Most teens can name at least one video game character. Many have a favorite video game, or a favorite scene, level, or moment from one. A few might have their own ideas for a game and wonder how they can create one.

At the core of all digital tools are programs. Programs are written and compiled as code using one or more computer languages. Computer science courses can increase one's understanding of how digital processes work, for storytelling or any application.

USING DIGITAL STORY TOOLS

Programming is rapidly becoming a critical component in education alongside math and reading.

Anyone who wants to create computer games or computer animation should study programming. Learning how to work with scripts makes creating these types of stories easier.

Even without programming skills, there are tools available for making games. Many are free and require only payment of a license fee if the resulting game is sold for money. Each software platform for game design has a community to help build, test, and even market games. Sometimes a commercial game publisher will buy the rights to an independently made game for commercial distribution.

Teacher and Student

For writers, a solid foundation in language skills, including vocabulary and grammar, is critical. Literature courses expose an aspiring writer to excellent stories that have stood the test of time. Reading good fiction helps one develop an understanding of character, plot, dialogue, setting, and other important story elements.

However, English literature is by no means the only subject from which one can draw. Meaningful stories speak to what it means to be alive or to be human. Other subjects represent these things, too. History, science, and art may seem different, but all attempt to make sense of the world. Even athletics seeks to measure the potential of the human form.

Students should keep this concept in mind when they do reports. A good report is more than a list of facts. Like a story, it is a sequence of ideas that build on each other. The writer can convey the information most effectively by connecting it to the audience's existing experience. Few students realize that when they present reports in school, they may be using one of the most powerful digital storytelling tools of today. Slide show presentation software, such as PowerPoint and Keynote, is a sharing platform known the world over. Sadly, its potential is underused. Far too many presentations are bullet point lists broken up by clip art or perhaps a graph. Such things have brought out many yawns in classrooms and business meetings for years.

A modern presentation merges words and images with animation and sound. These elements are not just glitz. They are a way to convey meaning and make transitions between ideas. Viewers should be led to the next frame. They should anticipate what is coming without knowing for certain what will be there. Slide show creation is a fundamental skill. The ability to create a strong digital presentation is beneficial in nearly every career field.

License to Hard Drive

An unfortunate side effect of the digital remix culture is the idea that because something can be copied easily, it's OK to do it without permission. Despite various forms of copyright protection, copying digital music, movies, and games is laughingly simple. Regardless of the ease of copying this material, it is still illegal theft. Software developers argue that they do not sell customers the software but rather a license to use the software. That license agreement puts limits on how the software can be used.

Digital storytellers work against their own interests by pirating software. Robbing artists and studios of payment for their work makes it harder for them to do more. Software companies aren't able to develop newer versions or additional software. Production companies can't fund new projects. Game studios go out of business. Pirating actually makes it harder for amateur digital storytellers to find a job or sell their work.

Even using an artist's song for background music on a slide show is likely against its copyright. Teens do this both because they are not aware of the law and because they believe they won't get caught. It's worth the time to learn how to do things properly. The remix culture has given rise to massive amounts of free-for-use or fair-use images, clips, sounds, songs, and more. By using these, creators can make something truly theirs—a product they can share or even sell guilt-free.

Join the Club

Beyond classwork, many school groups use digital tools in their activities. Working together on projects lets people learn from one another. In addition, schools might lend resources to a group that they wouldn't to an individual. A journalism class or club might get access to a video camera and video editing equipment, for instance.

Many schools involve students in publishing the school newspaper or yearbook. Students must present school and current events in an engaging way. Presenting the news requires strong writing and a good layout. Journalists must capture readers' attention enough to follow a story across jumps to later pages. Programs such as QuarkXPress, InDesign, and Publisher allow creative arrangement of text and images across pages and columns. Today's student reporters might also contribute to a school Web site. Students can learn to

Many schools and libraries provide access to hardware devices too costly for many students, sometimes even loaning or leasing laptops or video equipment to them.

arrange the content for Web viewing. With all of these school publications, the finished products are concrete items a student can save for a later portfolio.

Fiction writers have options, too. Book clubs are a good way to learn how fiction is structured and how writing techniques can aid a story. Writing clubs give writers a chance to share their own work with others. They may read their work aloud and listen to how it sounds. Club members can give feedback to help make one's writing stronger through revision. Modern writers should not be afraid to edit. Making changes to prose on a word processor is easy. People can also save multiple versions of their work as they develop a piece. The teacher or mentor for the group might also know of places to submit finished works for possible awards or publication.

Theater provides an early opportunity for students to tell another person's story but play with their own ideas in interpreting and presenting it.

A drama club can be great help to future fiction writers, playwrights, and screenwriters. Acting scenes can help students develop a feel for dialogue and character interaction. With digital video cameras and editing software readily available, storytellers can also work on film editing. Finding the heart of the story and cutting out the unnecessary parts are important skills.

The Larger Classroom

Many states offer young writers' programs, including camps, workshops, seminars, retreats, and contests. Similarly, a number of colleges offer programs for young writers. Participants can get instruction from college professors, use campus resources, and get a feel for the college atmosphere.

Online workshops and projects such as National Novel Writing Month, or NaNoWriMo, provide this experience without having to travel. Each November, people around the world challenge themselves to write a novel of at least fifty thousand words in thirty days. Online forums, challenges, and resources help writers meet their goals. While it is primarily an online event, many writers engage in work sessions with others in their area. "Winning" NaNoWriMo really means having a finished draft of a novel to work with. Still, NaNoWriMo sponsors provide heavily discounted site subscriptions, software, or publishing tools to both participants and winners. Afterward agents, editors, and publishers offer to look at finished novels for possible book publication.

The NaNoWriMo Young Writer's Program recorded participation of more than ninety-eight thousand K–12 students for 2012's NaNoWriMo. About 40 percent of those students were in high school. Information on how to join future efforts can be found at http://www.nanowrimo.org/en/ywp.

The Next Step

High school doesn't last forever. Whatever comes next must be earned. Telling one's own story is a challenging, but important, part of the process. The skills and experience that one gains in high school can make it easier. Completing a full-scale project like a novel, play, or working computer game shows perseverance on a college application. A series of published columns in the school newspaper or a short film might be work samples for a potential employer.

Military recruiters also value good communication, language, and technical skills. All potential recruits must take an entrance exam. High scores on the language and reading comprehension sections plus additional skills may qualify a recruit for enlistment bonuses, advanced training, and higher-paying jobs. All branches of the military use linguists, copywriters, public relations specialists, and other storytellers. These positions can be an attractive option and can be pursued even after a job or college.

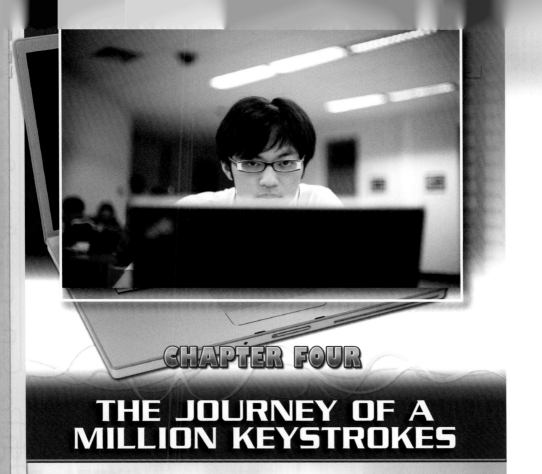

CHAPTER FOUR

THE JOURNEY OF A MILLION KEYSTROKES

Staying on the cutting edge of any field is difficult. This is especially true of digital tools and technologies. As new devices appear, people change the way they use electronics. The standard software in a field might be completely different five or ten years later.

Even so, there are standard types of software a digital storyteller should understand. Most of the time, the end user does not care what software a writer used. However, once a writer begins working with others, he or she may need to use the same software that they do.

The Toolbox

Most people are familiar with basic word processing programs such as Word and Pages. Such programs allow for notes, corrections, revisions, and more alongside the text. They have templates available that match the styles for movie and television scripts. Footnote and endnote features provide additional information and aid in writing nonfiction.

Sometimes the software a writer uses merely enhances an existing word processor. Plug-ins for Microsoft Word can expand its capabilities. For instance, EndNote keeps track of source materials and automatically creates bibliography entries for them.

For playwrights and screenwriters, knowledge of screenwriting software such as Final Draft and Movie

Software tools for digital storytelling allow creators to store, organize, and combine music, video, and text.

Magic is a must. These programs format stories to industry standards and include tools for tracking a story or characters. Some even have elements to aid in filming the story, such as identifying all the scenes that take place in the same location.

Fiction and nonfiction writers alike tend to do a lot of research and keep notes on what they plan to write. Heavy-duty writing programs such as Scrivener and Ulysses act as a writing desk. There are places to copy Web pages and information from the Internet, virtual notebooks for keeping character biographies, tools for organizing and changing scenes, and more.

Multimedia plays a large role in digital stories. Learning how to lay out text and images is helpful. InDesign and QuarkXpress are good for printed materials, but less so for the Web. Web pages are created using a mixture of computer languages. Creating one from scratch requires an understanding of HTML, CSS, Java, and more. Luckily, ready-made Web tools such as Kompozer and iWeb shield content providers from this process. People with more programming knowledge can try making animations, interactive cartoons, or games using Flash or HTML5.

Visual storytellers can also display static images on Flickr or Instagram. YouTube offers hosting for video clips, scenes, and short films. Facebook is a workable platform for combining pictures, sound, and video together into a single feed. So is WordPress, which can use add-on themes and tools for specific kinds of content.

Collaboration Tools

The Internet also allows real-time collaboration among people any distance apart. Google Docs is one well-known tool. The active document is hosted in "the cloud," which is a third party's remote file server. Each user sees the document on his or her screen and can make changes. Anything added, deleted, or changed takes place for everyone. One person may write a paragraph and another might add to it or correct a mistake. For documents that need regular input from other people, cloud tools are a huge time-saver. They have become so popular that Microsoft has moved its entire Office suite of programs onto the cloud.

One of the more impressive works to emerge from the sharing culture of the Internet is a film called *Project London*. The high-quality futuristic science-fiction movie contains heavy use of computer animation and digital effects. The film itself, however, cost almost nothing to make. The writing, acting, props, music, special effects, and digital retouches were done completely through volunteer work. Hundreds of people from around the Web worked together to build a complete film from almost nothing.

Notches on the Pencil

To tell stories for a living, one must have a collection of strong finished pieces ready. Gathering a portfolio of one's best work can help applications for college, work, and even artist grants. A good portfolio does more than show that an applicant is creative. It also shows that the creator has experience and has made the effort to present his or her work in a professional way.

 Digital portfolio works must be engaging, but the presenter should also make sure they can be accessed at a moment's notice without crashing.

Any work that has appeared in a publication is a good place to start. Poems, essays, news stories, or fiction chosen for magazines, newspapers, or literary journals can be photocopied or clipped. Digitally published work can be trickier. Text-only pieces can be printed out as word-processed documents. Pieces with images that can be printed at high resolution can also be reproduced on paper. Slideshows, video clips, and other multimedia projects should be saved on a CD-ROM or DVD. Anything else available on the Web should be noted on an application with a Web address. Screenshots should not be used because printouts lose the impact that a well-designed Web page has.

For any application, one should be sure to follow any and all guidelines set by the reviewer. Any mistakes, such as including too many works or failing to use proper formatting, can get an application thrown out. Scripts and essays in particular often have very specific margins, footnoting, and font requirements.

QUICK TIP Working in a digital medium usually means having work displayed online. Digital artists have to be careful as to how they represent themselves anyplace online. Employers might look for additional work or information about them. Any photos, forum posts, or inappropriate displays they find on social media or elsewhere could keep a person from getting a job.

It's not a bad idea to have more than one portfolio ready to go. For example, an applicant hoping for a career in journalism might have one collection tailored toward reporting jobs. It might demonstrate writing strength, attention to detail, and mastery of form. Another portfolio might focus on reviews and feature writing in a particular area. For instance, someone might want write mainly about music. That portfolio might include concert or album reviews, band interviews, an essay about the Beatles' influence on today's "boy band" pop groups, and a PowerPoint presentation on concert attendance versus record sales.

Service with a Simile

People who might not have contemplated a job in the military might wish to reconsider after getting additional education or training. All branches of the military need people who can string words, images, and ideas together effectively. The military has its own magazines, book presses, news outlets, video networks, blog channels, and more. It also has a healthy Web presence, with its own .mil suffix. The armed forces need compelling content as much as any other company or business. Service members who create such content not only get real-world job training, but good pay and military benefits such as college tuition or tuition repayment. *(continued on next page)*

In the military, important information is presented quickly and accurately, often using state-of-the-art technology.

[continued from previous page]

Learning or growing up with a second or third language can bring extra opportunities. The military has an English language mastery requirement because all of its instruction manuals and other important documents are in English. However, the U.S. military has operations around the world. Being able to express ideas in spoken word or print bilingually is an advantage in communicating on the military's behalf.

Being part of a military unit also provides insight into a life that only a soldier can truly understand. It is hard for someone outside the military to write about the military and sound authentic. Hands-on experience with the equipment, weaponry, locations, structure, and operations can give future stories the accurate details that make them realistic.

College Connections

As in high school, college students should pursue the subjects they are most enthusiastic about. Enthusiasm can only help one's work. English courses can improve writing skills, but they won't make anyone a writer without knowledge of other subjects. As a trip to the college bookstore shows, any field can be written about in depth.

To that end, coursework can become a source of story material. The notes, research, essays, and other work assigned can be saved and recycled into original stories. If a professor is impressed with an assignment, he or she might submit it to an academic or department journal. Student reports, stories, and scientific findings regularly appear in such places.

Between classes and homework, it can be hard to find time to work on personal creative projects. It helps to work with others to stay motivated. Most college campuses have numerous clubs for a wide range of interests, such as videography, writing, drama, or computer animation. Students work together and push each other to finish projects. A group leader or mentor can help showcase finished works.

Making time to write or work creatively should be like making time to eat, exercise, or catch a favorite television program. Little bits of regular progress can pay off over time. Even if it is only for a few hours on the weekend, it's important to keep working at it. The sense of accomplishment at the end of a successful project will be worth it.

Collaboration allows people to bring a combination of skills and experience from which everyone can benefit and learn.

In fact, the most helpful job-landing tool a person has upon college graduation may not even be the degree. The projects, theses, or writings created on the path to graduation can be even more valuable. One of the benefits of working on projects like animations, video shorts, multimedia clips, or games while in college is the ability to use college resources. Those resources may not be available again until after landing a job in a workplace that has them. Students should take full advantage of their enrollment to show what they can do with these tools.

TECH TOOLS

Nothing is worse than having hours of work disappear. Keep important files safe by making backups and saving regularly while working. Flash drives can be helpful for storing projects, but they need to be kept in a safe place that is easy to remember. Cloud hosting services can offer space on their services and some, like Dropbox, are free. Additional programs can synch up multiple storage locations so that the most recent files are shared everywhere.

The Human Network

There's no substitute for experience. While gaining experience, however, it's a good idea to network with people who have related experience. A person's professional network can never grow too large. For many people, that network starts with teachers and professors. Attending workshops and seminars is another great way to meet experienced professionals. There may also be people in the community doing the jobs one might want to learn. Many of the people who work for newspapers, television news, regional magazines, or local blogs are willing to give newcomers advice.

If a business seems like the perfect place to work, it may be worth asking about internships. An intern is an assistant, often unpaid, who works at a job in exchange for learning about the industry. A person might take an internship at a television station to learn how to edit video footage into a series of stories for television or the Web. This can lead to a job later, or at least a valuable reference.

High schools and colleges often have job resource centers. Guidance and career counselors can put students in touch with employers whose needs may match their skills or goals. These centers can also help with applications or portfolios. Staff can help students make their submissions meet the requirements for grants, awards, higher education, and other opportunities. They also are excellent coaches for preparing for job, college, or graduate school interviews.

CHAPTER FIVE

TURNING THE PAGE

The creative rush to work on a project can be very strong. Yet few people can afford to throw everything else aside to focus on a project. Work issues, family issues, and even health issues have to find a balance against creating and sharing a story. It helps, then, to find a line of work that supports that creativity as much as possible.

Possible Jobs

There are a wide variety of jobs for someone who has a way with words. Journalists might work for newspapers or magazines, both in print and online. Popular Web sites may need reporters or bloggers. Businesses want people who can use text to draw attention from search engines. Most companies need public relations people who can be their voice online. Celebrities and entertainers use publicists as filters between themselves and the media. Movies and television shows use whole rooms of writers to collaborate on scripts. Authors still provide reading material in print and e-book forms for hungry readers.

For an artist, the Web is a limitless gallery. Today, artists, cartoonists, and graphic novelists don't even need to scan art onto a computer. Products like the Wacom tablet give artists a broad range of brush tools to illustrate directly on the screen. Images can remain still or be given life with animation tools. Digital artists can import their work into animation studios to make cartoons, television shows, Web series, films, motion comics, or games. Creative professionals in advertising or marketing can use these tools to make eye-catching ads.

Those who like to work behind a camera can pair their images with a writer's words to make stunning books, catalog material for retail Web sites, or engaging magazine articles. Videographers can record, edit, and add special effects to make films, shows, or commercials. A little video wizardry can be used to make entertaining video blogs and humorous sketches.

Programmers can tell their stories in a variety of ways. Besides inventing all of the digital tools in the world, programmers can be highly creative. Their engines create the worlds behind game developers' most cinematic titles. They form the foundation for animated

 Programmers are responsible for designing a game's engine: the rules, behaviors, and properties that the objects in the game follow.

movie classics from companies such as Pixar and DreamWorks. Even working alone, a programmer can create a mobile game in less time than it might take a writer to finish a novel.

 A Pixar animator named William Joyce merged three media to create *The Fantastic Flying Books of Mr. Morris Lessmore*. It exists as an Oscar-winning short film, a physical book, and an application for mobile devices. Each version expresses the story in different ways that take advantage of its medium.

DIY Y/N?

Making the jump from spare-time to part-time or full-time storytelling can be challenging. In some cases, however, a person working on a fun side project accidentally finds huge success. Luca Redwood made his simple, addictive game *10000000* while at home with his new-born child. After one rave review on a widely read site, it quickly got over fifty thousand downloads with no other advertising at all. The game, in which players train to outrun a dungeon's traps, has become a top seller in twenty-five countries.

There is less pressure in working on one's own projects as a hobby. There is no real deadline, and it can be done as time permits. The creator has the security of his or her regular job. Unfortunately, a hobby project can

The Fantastic Flying Books of Mr. Morris Lessmore, created by filmmakers William Joyce *(left)* and Brandon Oldenburg *(right)*, told its Academy Award–winning story using animation and music but no dialogue.

also be ignored for long stretches of time or never get finished. It might be less relevant or interesting when it is finally completed.

If a side project begins to invade the day job, though, it might be time to move to freelancing. Taking freelance jobs is a good way to build contacts and get some experience in the field. With the ability to work from any location over the Web, freelancers can take jobs from employers across the country and beyond. Plus, in a shaky economy, businesses are outsourcing jobs that were once full-time.

The Internet offers help to freelancers. Some of the most valuable tools are community sites such as FreelanceWriting .com and RedRoom.com. People can get leads and advice for finding jobs, search for collaborators, and share their projects.

Anyone seeking to write or present stories for a living should have some already prepared. The quality of the work will speak as loud as or louder than an interview. Everything in one's portfolio should be free from errors. It should speak to the creativity and craft of the author. A person looking at these work samples must be engaged and not bored.

In addition, a portfolio submission should match the needs of the recipient. Any guidelines regarding size, formatting, genre, and even computer file type must be followed. An applicant should become familiar enough with the company to tailor his or her submission to the nature of the business's work. A magazine article should be a similar length and written for the same audience as the articles in the publication that one is submitting to.

Before hiring someone, many businesses also ask applicants to generate a work sample on a specific topic. This shows them that the job candidate can address the topic on the level they want. It also lets them see whether the person can deliver quality work in a short amount of time. Even with a quick turnaround, any samples produced on demand should be proofread and edited as any other work would. Programs should be debugged as thoroughly as possible.

Playing Well with Others

While there are solo artists making a living from their craft, few digital storytellers work alone. Learning how to work on a team is a critical job skill. The Internet age brings with it some standard expectations for working together online.

Today, people carry their smartphones and Web devices everywhere. Fair or not, this means employers and fellow workers may expect quick responses. It's all right to respond to e-mail with a short answer quickly and a fuller answer later. This lets the sender know the first e-mail was received and gives him or her a time frame for a full response.

Since work submissions can be instantly sent or uploaded, some people push deadlines too far. While work should not be rushed, there is no harm in beating a deadline. There are always computer problems, network outages, and other tech problems to fear. A power outage on the day of a deadline isn't a great excuse.

You Mean My Fan Fiction Is Worth Something?

Fan fiction involves writing stories about characters that are someone else's property. The copyright holder might be the author or publisher of a book series, a movie studio, or a television network. Nearly every successful story franchise has an active fan fiction community. Writing in this genre is a common exercise for beginning storytellers, since they have the benefit of established story elements to build on. Some writers advise storytellers to avoid writing fan fiction and consider it beneath them. However, there is a specific case in which a well-written piece of fan fiction can be the stepping-stone to a writing career.

Television writers are required to have one or more "spec" scripts to show a possible employer. A spec script is a properly formatted script for an episode of a television show. Writers typically submit a script for a show that is similar to the one they are hoping to write for. A writer trying to get a job working on *Pretty Little Liars* might submit a spec script for *Gossip Girl*, for instance. Spec scripts allow writers to demonstrate that they can create original material that is entertaining, yet true to the characters and show.

Filmmakers can similarly set themselves apart by showcasing their technical skills. The popular *Star Wars* films have motivated many special effects wizards to create film-faithful lightsaber duels for YouTube. Likewise, comic book artists regularly create images of iconic heroes who have been interpreted by many storytellers in the past. Such creations can be a valuable part of one's portfolio.

Patience and professionalism are required at all times. Tweets and texts have led to regular use of short-hand in writing. However, work e-mails should use correct spelling, grammar, and punctuation. They should avoid informal acronyms. Writing should be polite, and appropriate time should be given before sending a follow-up.

Privacy is another big concern. Even though work is being shared, it may also need to be kept secret. Work done for one company cannot be used in a portfolio or work sample without permission. A work in progress should never be used. Privacy restrictions are usually spelled out in a work-for-hire contract. Freelancers, part-time employees, and full-time employees often have to sign one before beginning work on a project.

Alongside privacy concerns are security concerns. Company assets such as software, files, texts, and art are valuable. If any of this data is stolen, lost, or shared, it can hurt the company financially. Someone who allows data theft to occur, even accidentally, can be fired or even prosecuted. All passwords to company e-mail accounts, servers, and databases must be kept private.

Another danger is that the story itself could be revealed. Few things are more damaging than having the ending to a film, Web series, or game leaked to the Internet before release.

Warnings aside, using the vast potential of digital tools for storytelling can be a fun, amazing experience. Getting to share a new story, or tell a familiar story in a new way, carries on an ancient tradition. To be able to make a living at it isn't hard to imagine. But it will take vision to create the next chapter of digital storytelling, and the one after that.

GLOSSARY

agent A person hired to represent a person's work and market his or her talent.

aggregator An application that collects a specific type of information or content from multiple Internet sources and consolidates it for viewing.

collaborate To work jointly with others.

content The main substance of work found on a Web site.

debug To remove errors from a computer program.

freelancer A self-employed person who sells his or her services for specific assignments, rather than working continuously for one employer.

genre A particular category or style of art.

grant Money given to a person or organization in order to fund a worthy project.

interactive Requiring actions or input from the user.

license Permission to use software or other assets in exchange for a fee or a specific kind of use.

mash-up An audio recording that combines samples from other recordings, usually from different musical styles.

platform A means of delivering a digital experience.

publisher A company that takes on the cost of distributing something in exchange for profiting from the sales.

revenue The income from a business enterprise or other source.

seminar A focused gathering dedicated to exchanging ideas on a particular topic.

static Unmoving or unchanging.

suite A group of software programs intended to work together on a computer.

FOR MORE INFORMATION

Bay Area Video Coalition (BAVC)
2727 Mariposa Street, 2nd Floor
San Francisco, CA 94110
(415) 861-3282
Web site: http://www.bavc.org
This organization empowers independent media makers
to develop and share diverse stories through art,
education, and technology. Its youth programs help
young people increase their storytelling, social jus-
tice, and media arts skills. Participants develop
their artistic talents while receiving advanced training in digital media production.

Canadian Film Centre (CFC)
2489 Bayview Avenue
Toronto, ON M2L 1A8
Canada
(416) 445-1446
Web site: http://www.cfccreates.com
Created in 1995, the CFC is part education center and
part think tank. It brings industry leaders and
creative minds together to anticipate and create
new innovations in a variety of media. At the
forefront of digital storytelling trends, the CFC
has had a number of noteworthy projects, including a full-length, interactive feature film called
Late Fragment.

Center for Digital Storytelling
1250 Addison Street, Suite 104
Berkeley, CA 94702
(510) 548-2065
Web site: http://www.storycenter.org
This center assists youth and adults in using digital
media tools to craft, record, and share meaningful
stories from their lives. Its unique workshops assist
participants in producing short, first-person narratives that can be presented in a variety of
traditional and social media formats.

DigiPen Institute of Technology
9931 Willows Road NE
Redmond, WA 98052
(866) 478-5236
Web site: https://www.digipen.edu
DigiPen is a specialized, for-profit college focusing on
computer interactive technologies. It offers degree
programs in game programming, game design, and
fine arts and multimedia production and engineer-
ing. The school offers workshops and courses in
which middle school and high school students can
learn about game theory and design.

International Storytelling Center (ISC)
116 W. Main Street
Jonesborough, TN 37659
(800) 952-8392
Web site: http://www.storytellingcenter.net

This nonprofit organization works to provide the knowledge, experiences, and tools to help individuals, organizations, and communities tap into the power of stories. In particular, it teaches people how to discover, craft, and share stories that celebrate personal, community, and cultural heritage.

National Institute for Technology in Liberal Education (NITLE)
Southwestern University
1001 East University Avenue
Georgetown, TX 78626
(512) 863-1603
Web site: http://www.nitle.org

The NITLE advocates and researches digital storytelling methods, and has created many standard definitions used in the field. While it focuses primarily on helping educators use digital storytelling tools, it also runs seminars and workshops for all ages designed to give people the tools to complete a storytelling project.

Web Sites

Due to the changing nature of Internet links, Rosen Publishing has developed an online list of Web sites related to the subject of this book. This site is updated regularly. Please use this link to access the list:

http://www.rosenlinks.com/DCB/DST

FOR FURTHER READING

Barr, Chris. *The Yahoo! Style Guide: The Ultimate Sourcebook for Writing, Editing, and Creating Content for the Digital World*. New York, NY: Yahoo!/St. Martin's Griffin, 2010.

Benke, Karen. *Rip the Page! Adventures in Creative Writing*. Boston, MA: Trumpeter Books, 2010.

Culver, Sherri Hope, and James A. Seguin. *Media Career Guide: Preparing for Jobs in the 21st Century*. 8th ed. Boston, MA: Bedford/St. Martins, 2012.

Gilbert, Sara. *Write Your Own Article: Newspaper, Magazine, Online* (Write Your Own). Minneapolis, MN: CompassPoint Books, 2009.

Hicks, Troy. *Crafting Digital Writing: Composing Texts Across Media and Genres*. Portsmouth, NH: Heinemann, 2013.

Korolenko, Michael, and Bruce Wolcott. *Storytelling and Design: Media Literacy for the Digital Age*. Boston, MA: Pearson Custom Publishing, 2006.

Kurtz, Scott, et al. *How to Make Webcomics*. 2nd ed. Berkeley, CA: Image Comics, 2008.

Lambert, Joe. *Digital Storytelling: Capturing Lives, Creating Community*. 4th ed. New York, NY: Routledge, 2013.

Orr, Tamra B. *Creating Multimedia Presentations* (Digital and Information Literacy). New York, NY: Rosen Publishing, 2010.

Sethi, Maneesh. *Game Programming for Teens*. 3rd ed. Boston, MA: Course Technology, 2009.

BIBLIOGRAPHY

Alexander, Bryan. *The New Digital Storytelling: Creating Narratives with New Media*. Santa Barbara, CA: Praeger, 2011.

Crace, John. "The Teen Bloggers Who Took Over the Internet." *The Guardian*, September 8, 2009. Retrieved December 18, 2012 (http://www.guardian.co.uk).

Fam, Mariam. "Free of Qaddafi's Grip, Young Libyans in Benghazi Find a Voice." Bloomberg.com, May 25, 2011. Retrieved January 21, 2013 (http://www.bloomberg.com).

Faraday, Owen. "How a Bedroom Developer's 'Ugly Little Game' Became an App Store Hit." Wired.co.uk, September 4, 2012. Retrieved February 4, 2013 (http://www.wired.co.uk).

FoxNews.com. "10 Most Famous Kid Critics and Cooks." August 14, 2012. Retrieved January 17, 2013 (http://www.foxnews.com).

Gillette, Felix. "Digital Media Dreams, Elusive Profits." Businessweek.com, October 25, 2012. Retrieved December 19, 2012 (http://www.businessweek.com).

Goodman, Abbey. "Tavi Gevinson May Take Over the World While You Read This." CNN.com, January 2, 2013. Retrieved January 13, 2013 (http://www.cnn.com).

Kornblum, Janet. "Teens Wear Their Hearts on Their Blog." *USA Today*, October 30, 2005. Retrieved December 18, 2012 (http://usatoday30.usatoday.com).

Loechner, Jack. "Teen Media Behavior; Texting, Talking, Socializing, TV Watching, Mobiling." MediaPost.com, June 23, 2011. Retrieved December 18, 2012 (http://www.mediapost.com).

Lunden, Ingrid. "McAfee: Sneaky Teens Surf on PCs More Than Mobile, Facebook Rules Over All Other Social Networks." TechCrunch.com, June 25, 2012. Retrieved December 19, 2012 (http://techcrunch.com).

Maffeo, Lauren. "The Best Apps, Communities & Tools for Writers and Journalists." TheNextWeb.com, September 29, 2012. Retrieved December 20, 2012 (http://thenextweb.com).

McNaughton, Marissa. "Social Networking Stats: Nearly 90% of U.S. Teens on Facebook, #RLTM Scoreboard." TheRealtimeReport.com, June 29, 2012. Retrieved December 18, 2012 (http://therealtimereport.com).

Miller, Carolyn Handler. *Digital Storytelling: A Creator's Guide to Interactive Entertainment.* 2nd ed. Burlington, MA: Focal Press, 2008.

Miller, Rebecca. "Dramatic Growth: LJ's Second Annual E-book Survey." TheDigitalShift.com, October 12, 2011. Retrieved December 18, 2012 (http://www.thedigitalshift.com).

Mosher, Chip. "ComiXology: iTunes #3 Top-Grossing iPad App of 2012." ComiXology Blog, December 17, 2012. Retrieved December 18, 2012 (http://blog.comixology.com).

Owen, Laura Hazard. "Hearst: 'Nearly 800,000' Digital U.S. Subs, Short of 1 Million Goal." PaidContent.org. January 2, 2013. Retrieved January 5, 2013 (http://paidcontent.org).

PublishingPerspectives.com. "Looking at US E-book Statistics and Trends." October 3, 2012. Retrieved December 19, 2012 (http://publishingperspectives.com).

Rodriguez, Rachel. "From iReporter to CNNer (and Beyond)." CNN.com, August 11, 2011. Retrieved January 21, 2013 (http://articles.cnn.com).

Tynan, Dan. "Meet the Whiz Kids: 10 Overachievers Under 21." *PCWorld*, March 9, 2008. Retrieved January 17, 2013 (http://www.pcworld.com).

Varela, Anelia. "There's More to a Career in Writing Than Being a Journalist or Novelist." Guardian.co.uk, January 24, 2012. Retrieved December 20, 2012 (http://careers.guardian.co.uk).

Walsh, Declan. "Malala Yousafzai, Shot by Pakistani Taliban, Is Discharged from Hospital." *New York Times*, January 4, 2013. Retrieved January 19, 2013 (http://www.nytimes.com).

Whelan, Debra Lau. "More School Libraries Offer E-books; Increased Demand, Rise in Circulation." *School Library Journal*, October 13, 2011. Retrieved December 18, 2012 (http://www.schoollibraryjournal.com).

Whitney, Daisy. "Popular But Not Profitable." TVWeek.com, March 2008. Retrieved January 31, 2013 (http://www.tvweek.com).

INDEX

About the Author

Jason Glaser has had over seventy works published in various forms, including a children's picture e-book and a multimedia chapbook of poetry about video games. As the featured author at the Fifth Annual Language Arts Festival at Wayne State University in 2009, he presented a keynote speech titled "How a Generation of Texters Might Save the English Language."

Photo Credits

Cover, p. 1 © iStockphoto.com/MiquelMunill (laptop and hands), © iStockphoto.com/EricVega (iPad), © iStockphoto.com/pederk (camera); p. 4 (inset) © iStockphoto.com/Peter McKinnon; p. 6 Mark Bowden/E+/Getty Images; pp. 9, 48 © AP Images; p. 11 © iStockphoto.com/svariophoto; p. 13 (inset) © iStockphoto.com /AIMSTOCK; p. 14 St. Martin's Griffin/AP Images; p. 17 © Richard Perry/The New York Times/Redux Pictures; p. 19 © iStockphoto.com/Andrea Zanchi; p. 22 Bryan Steffy/WireImage /Getty Images; p. 25 (inset) © iStockphoto.com/mediaphotos; p. 27 Dikiiy/Shutterstock.com; p. 28 © Pat Vasquez-Cunningham /Albuquerque Journal/ZUMA Press; p. 31 Tom Grill/Photographer's Choice/Getty Images; p. 32 Comstock/Thinkstock; p. 35 (inset) © iStockphoto.com/Mingzhe Zhang; p. 36 © iStockphoto.com /Chris Schmidt; p. 39 karelnoppe/Shutterstock.com; p. 41 U.S. Navy photo by Photographer's Mate 1st Class Aaron Ansarov; p. 43 Goodluz/Shutterstock.com; p. 46 (inset) Maxim Blinkov /Shutterstock.com; p. 49 Robyn Beck/AFP/Getty Images; cover and interior pages background patterns and graphics © iStockphoto.com/Ali Mazraie Shadi, © iStockphoto.com/MISHA, © iStockphoto.com/Paul Hill, © iStockphoto.com/Charles Taylor, © iStockphoto.com/Daniel Halvorson, © iStockphoto.com/Jeffrey Sheldon; additional interior page design elements © iStockphoto .com/Lisa Thornberg (laptop pp. 4, 13, 25, 35, 46), © iStockphoto .com/abu (computer mouse).

Designer: Nelson Sa; Editor: Andrea Sclarow Paskoff; Photo Researcher: Karen Huang